I ASK MY MOTHER
TO SING

A Wesleyan Chapbook

I ASK MY MOTHER TO SING

mother poems of
Li-Young Lee

edited by Oliver Egger

Wesleyan University Press
Middletown, Connecticut

Wesleyan University Press
Middletown, Connecticut 06459
www.weslpress.org

ISBN 978-0-8195-0203-2

Cover Image: ***Madonna con il Bambino*** ©
Veneranda Fabbrica del Duomo di Milano

For my mother, the first mystery

CONTENTS

Introduction: **Her Gaze**

A composite of perspectives from two interviews conducted in January 2025 with Li-Young Lee

It's impossible for me to talk about my mother. She comes before everything, before words, before the world, and before words for the world. Before syntax.

> My mother is difficult to think about and to talk about because she was one of the most mysterious people I've ever met. She means so many things to me and at so many levels, at so many scales, in so many dimensions, that I feel eternally as if I'm her subject. I'm second person to her first personhood, somehow.

>> She saw me before I saw her. And she taught me to pray. And she reminded me all the time to pray. She said, "Only pray. Nothing else makes sense, just pray." And what is prayer? I've been asking my whole life.

There is an inner room in me, and I think my mother either helped me build that room, or I inherited it from her. One of the early introductions to this inner room was when, as a child, I found her crying to herself. By allowing me into her grief, I found this inner room inside myself.

> All of my sentence patterns more than likely have imprinted upon them the patterns she pressed into my very body and soul while I lay inside her, growing, listening, a pattern growing inside of her patterns of happiness and sadness, hope and despair, hunger and satiety, waking, dreaming, or sleeping, love and fear.

For all I know, her face lies behind every face I see. My mother's face is the first face. She is the first voice. The face and the voice before everything. I can't contemplate what comes before everything. That's like thinking about God. That's impossible.

> But Poetry is impossible. Poetry is impossible because poetry is thinking which contemplates its own source, words spoken within hearing of their precondition: silence. Poetry is words which find their source not in other words, but in human listening and its silence. And that's why we who practice poetry continually practice turning a line back to the beginning. Writing poetry is impossible. Thinking about poetry is impossible. Two impossibles: poetry and my mother. I have my beginning in both. Syntax and mother, both come before the world. Poetry made the world. Poetry is the language of creation. Poetry is the language of ultimate reality. Poetic logic is the logic of creation, the logic of God, the logic of ecstasy, since ecstasy is that process by which any phenomenon emerges, by which any and all worlds are manifest. Poetry is in the world but not of the world. Poetry makes the world.

My mother never assimilated. She never quite learned English. She learned enough just to get her through to about the age of 60. And then she totally just gave up and spoke very little English. And before that, she spoke very halting English. She spoke only Chinese with us. She wanted to ensure that we spoke our Chinese. She was a symbol for me, a living symbol of old China and of the inner world of family.

The family was Chinese. And because of that, America remained outside. America always felt like it was not quite home.

So many things that happened to her, terrible things just happened to her. Things like a mob coming to her house and destroying it. She wasn't going to have a say there. She wasn't going to put her foot down and go, "Okay, I'm asserting my power." No, no, no, no. You're going to say, "How small can I make myself so I don't get in the way?"

I keep thinking about the nature of the mother, and I keep thinking that she was a perfect mother if that means she was the bearer of all things. She literally bore all things. And the nature of that is the same as how to make a poem. The poem is a receptacle of consciousness and unconsciousness. So, it's a maternal practice, and it's a practice of the mind and the mind retiring and nursing.

Home was where my mother's audience began. And I grew up in her audience. She had a very loving, very capacious, and very blank audience that allowed for a lot. She was a very tolerant, very loving, and very private woman. And this privacy she instilled in me.

In the beginning was poetry. And without poetry, there is neither cosmos nor world, and certainly no person or persons. No figures, no mother, no son.

There was a bipolarity to her. She went from a total sanctification, intelligence, and understanding to just total grief and despair. There's a similar bipolarity in art, in the poem. The poem is an altar. This altar, traditionally, is the place a human being makes exchanges with the divine realms: the dead, the upper worlds, the lower worlds. That symbol of the altar to my mind, that's what the blank page is, that's what the horizon of the pages is. The poem invites the greatest contradictions and solves them without reducing any of the elements to some sort of incoherent soup. That, to me, is the great poem.

This idea of the inner room, the inner sanctum, the place for prayer, these are all feminine ideas. I think my mother set the terms in the same way that the feminine sets the terms in poetry. The way the sonnet sets the terms. Fourteen is a feminine number, directly related to the feminine body, and it was invented, legend has it, by a woman who set the terms for a male to fulfill during the times of the troubadours. This is prior to Petrarch, who stole it from the troubadours. So this idea that the feminine sets the terms is a founding principle of all myths and legends of the art forms that are deeply embedded in the structure of the lover and the beloved.

To think about my mother is to contemplate first things. First patterns. Cradles are made in her image. Poetry is the voice of infancy and the mind of innocence. But so are boats and entrances to temples and tombs made in her image. Poetry is the voice of ultimate experience and death. Poetry is the understanding of first and last things.

I never knew if I was trying to win my mother's heart or God's when I wrote poems.

There was always so much between us that was unclear. I wrote in order to clarify myself to her. I wanted her to see me clearly.

Her gaze on me and my gaze on her. I grew up in her gaze. That's what I mean by her audience: her gaze. She had a beautiful gaze. And she had a beautiful "Amen." She taught me how to pray.

When she was dying, I just crawled up onto her bed and didn't leave for, what was it, a month, two months? I don't even know how long. I should know. As she died, I just held her and held her and held her. And she kept confusing me for somebody else. My father. She turned into a baby. Her body was just riddled with bed sores. I was changing her bandages three or four times a day. But man, she was a beautiful, beautiful person.

I Ask My Mother to Sing

She begins, and my grandmother joins her.
Mother and daughter sing like young girls.
If my father were alive, he would play
his accordion and sway like a boat.

I've never been in Peking, or the Summer Palace,
nor stood on the great Stone Boat to watch
the rain begin on Kuen Ming Lake, the picnickers
running away in the grass.

But I love to hear it sung;
how the waterlilies fill with rain until
they overturn, spilling water into water,
then rock back, and fill with more.

Both women have begun to cry.
But neither stops her song.

The Inheritance

Mother, your hair
has fallen
for the last time,
and I can't raise it up.
And I can't put it down.

I can't leave it on the ground.
The ground is too crowded with the living,
too teeming with the dead.

I can't store it in the sky. The sky's too full
of birds and clouds and airplanes.

And the seas are full of mountains
and creatures and ships coming and going.

And as long as earth turns,
all of the seasons are full of days.

There's no place to lay your hair down.

Sleep won't have it.
Your hair whispers too many secrets and stories.

Night doesn't want it.
There are no stars your hair won't swallow.

When you were alive,
you gathered it, bound it, and piled it,
to balance on the top of your head.
A small black urn, it shone.
Later, it shone white.

But your hair has come undone
once and for all time,
and what was one
now is many.

What started at your crown,
now has no beginning.

What stopped at your waist,
now has no end.
Now can't be collected or dispersed.
Now neither story nor song can comb or weigh.
Now has no measure or address.
Now can't be counted or left out.

And I can't carry it.
And I can't put it down.

The Blessed Knot

Look upon me, Love,
my mother said to God.

Love looked down,
God saw her,
and I was born

the first time.
Thats my mother's story.
And why wouldn't I believe her?
She gave me her body to eat,
she put the first words in my mouth,
and I sheltered in her gaze.

According to my mother,
I was planted in her heart,
I was cherished in her womb,
I was fostered at her breast
and reluctantly surrendered to the world,
in successive births.

She gazed upon me
in her arms and said, Love,
look at me.
But I couldn't see.
For days. For months. I couldn't see.
She called and called.
When I finally saw her,
I was born once more.

If what she says is true,
from that moment on, I must have only grown

in certainty her gaze
reached me from a forever far,
forever secret
place inside her I'd never chart.

My mother said, Amen.
My mother taught me to say, Amen.

Just above a whisper, in such trust
the prayerful one, in time
found missing, is never heard leaving.

Amen. So no one hears but God.
Amen. For no ears but God's.

And why wouldn't I trust her?
She carried me across two seas and four borders,
fleeing death by principalities and powers.

She taught me how to untie knots,
and she taught me to know when
to cut a knot with a knife.

And didn't I follow her voice and find her face?

Bless the knot
of my mother looking up
and silently calling out, Love,
and God looking down.

Bless the knot
of my mother looking down
and quietly calling out, Love,
and my looking up.

The Favorite

1. Little Idiot Lost

"Chanticleer!" my mother shouts,
calling my brother to supper.

I wonder when
my mother will call
my name.

"Songbird!" my mother shouts,
calling my sister
to the table.

"Many Trees!" she shouts.
"Blessing Who Stands!" she shouts.

When will my mother
call me?

"Excellent Strength!
Goddess of Wine!
Lady of the Ocean Waves for Hair!" she shouts,
calling her children to eat.

"No one touch the food," she says,
"until Little Idiot gets here."

I hope my mother calls me soon.
The food is already starting to get cold.

"Little Idiot!" she shouts.
"Little Idiot!" she cries.

"Where's Little Idiot?" she asks.

In one voice, they tell her,
"Little Idiot held up his heart
as a mirror to the moon.

Everybody knows you don't do that.
Never use your heart as a mirror
for inanimate objects.

The moon fell into the mirror,
lost itself inside, and that idiot
hid the mirror in his breast pocket.
Now he goes in the marketplace,
charging a peck for a peek."

"That's no way to find a wife!" shouts my mother.

"Little Idiot stole a giant boat.
He kicked out all the people and animals.
He said a prayer, and with a skeleton crew went sailing
to the end of the world. He peered over the edge,
and no one knows what he saw,
but he returned from there walking backwards
and repeating, All roads be blessed. Good-bye!"

"That's no way to become a man!" shouts my mother.

"Little Idiot!" she calls.
"Little Turd! Nobody eats
until that shit-fleck gets here," she says.

By now the food is cold.
No one knows where Little Idiot is.

We're all hungry.
And my mother still hasn't said my name.

2. *Little Idiot Found*

Mother, what do I care
about living and dying?
I saw the hummingbird.
I have seen the hummingbird.
I will see the hummingbird again.

What do I care about rich or poor,
what to eat, what to drink, what to wear?
I drank from Hummingbird's mouth.
I sat at Hummingbird's feet on a mountain of skulls,
and Hummingbird opened his heart to me,
a book of wonders,
and Hummingbird fed me those pages.

I saw Hummingbird get married.
I attended the wedding.
Death presided over the ceremony.
The exchange of vows between
that bride and groom creates the world.
What do I care about Time
or running out of time?
What do I care about profit and loss?

I watched Hummingbird enter the bridal chamber.
I watched Death seal the chamber doors
and a cloud descend upon it.
And then I saw Hummingbird fly out like lightning,
with Death between Hummingbird's teeth

and the firmament around his waist
separating the upper and lower waters.

Who cares how the world ends?
Hummingbird showed me the beginning and the end.

Why would I possibly worry
about living and dying?

Infant Longing

Because to God must be given
the things that belong to God
and to the world must be given
the things that belong to the world, I kiss you
with both lips, upper and lower.

Because the world keeps beginning
and ending the same way,
with the slaughter of the innocent,
with the massacre of the blameless,
and there's not a thing anyone can do.

O, who will roll the stone
from the mouth of the tomb for us?

I kiss you thus, because the world ended
with my mother walking among the slaughtered
to find her own.

I kiss you thus, because the world began with my mother
finding among the slaughtered her own
and burying them.

And when I was hungry and crying in her arms,
she stopped my mouth with her breast,
and she fed me her longing at the end of the world.

And when I wouldn't stop crying
in her arms, she bared her other breast
to my mouth, and she fed me
her longing at the beginning of the world.

It's like you kissing my mouth
to seal my mouth.

It's like you kissing my mouth
to open my mouth.

Like you kissing my mouth
to open my eyes.

Like you kissing my mouth
to close my eyes.

What's the difference
between these kisses?

Who will roll the stone
from the mouth of the tomb for us?
The round stone. The square tomb.

When we kiss,
when the upper and lower in you
meet the upper and lower in me,
and what is high is humbled
and what is low is raised,
when the round stone of time is rolled away
from the square space of earth,

you and I see what comes
before the beginning and after the end:
An infinite longing
moving over the face of the deep.

Pocket Catechism

Say the words:
On earth
as it is in heaven.

Say the words:
Love thy neighbor
as thyself.

Say the words:
And The Lord saw that it was good,
and it was good.

Say the words, said my father.
So I said the words.

Sing the words, said my mother.
So I sang the words.

But my sister said, Dance.
But I didn't know how to dance.
So my sister taught me.

Night said, Sleep.
But I didn't know how to sleep.
And I still don't know.

Day said, Rise. Work.
Sing for your mother.
Dance for your sister.
Say the words for your father.

So I sing the living waters.

So I dance the fallen angel.
So I say the words:
Mama may have.
Papa may have.
God bless the child that's got his own.

The Reaping

It's good to remember what my father remembered.

Blood on the doorposts,
blood on the lintels and thresholds.
That's how the world ends.
That's how the world begins.

It's good to remember what my mother remembered.

At the end of the world, you'll hear someone say,
"And I alone have escaped to tell you."
At the beginning of the world, you'll hear someone say,
"And I alone have escaped to tell you."

And the day will come
when it is necessary
to sacrifice the lamb.

For who will roll the round stone
from the square door of the tomb for us?

It's good to remember the end of the world.
It's good to remember the beginning of the world.

Therefore, I kiss the lintel of your forehead.
I kiss the threshold of your feet.
I kiss the doorposts of your shoulders and arms.

Therefore, on the day of the lamb,
I lay my square body
beneath your round body.

And I remember Boaz
leaned toward Ruth at mealtime
and said, "Come here and eat some bread,
and dip your morsel in the wine."

That too was the end of the world.
That too was the beginning of the world.

And I remember Ruth sat down beside the reapers,
and Boaz passed to her roasted grain,
and she ate until she was satisfied,
and she had some left over.

That too is how the world ends.
That too is how the world begins.

Love, we rolled. We threshed.
We chafed the grain and parched it.
Leave me to glean,
do not rebuke me.

Mother Comfort and Who

Little One, you can come out now.
The soldiers are gone.
They've had their fill of blood for today.

Mother, I saw God, and God was three
bare-chested men carrying machetes.

God's three bodies glistened
with sweat and spattered blood.
God's three breasts heaved, God's three mouths
open and panting from a morning of hard work,
killing and dismembering.

I'll come out
when the new moon comes out.

Little One, you can come out now.
The mob has moved on.
They've had their fill of rage for today.

Mother, I saw God and God was three.

And one third of God pointed with his finger and said,
Let's kill this one too.

And one third of God said,
No. Let him go.

And the last third of God
turned his face to me and said,
One day, you must return
to this country where you were born.

Mother, I'll come out
when the new stars come out.

Little One, wake up.
You've been dreaming again
about what happened so many years ago.

Mother, I'm awake.
I saw God and God was three men,
and the three men became three blades
turning this way and that way, dull on one side
and sharp on the other side.

And the three blades became three tongues.
And the three tongues are inside one cave.
And one tongue keeps saying, You must return
to where you were born.
And one keeps saying, Kill this one too.
And one keeps saying, Let him go.

Mother Deluxe

"We can't stay where we are,
and we don't know where else to go,"

is the first card my mother deals. We're playing
her deluxe edition of "Memories
from the 20th Century."

"Dead Baby," "Mystery Bundles," "Cleansing by Sacrifice."

Seven cards apiece and the object is to not die.

"Exodus," "Eyes Snatched Away,"
"Superstition at the Side of the Road."

All cards are good or bad depending on how you play them.
"Defeated by Wings," "Eating Forbidden Blood."

No card possesses inherent value.
"Among the Lepers," "Burial by the Solo River,"
"The Extracted Oil."

Every player begins in bondage.
Every player eventually dies. Everybody plays
whether they know or don't know they're playing.

Maybe this isn't a game.
Maybe it's the World Evening News.

Maybe this time I'll rescue my mother.
I can't tell if I thought that or if she said it.

Maybe this isn't the news.

Maybe this is a dream God is having
and somebody should wake Him.

Good boat, first boat, old boat, Mother,
my first night with you lasted nine months.
Our second night together is the rest of my life.

Asking Forgiveness

Forgive me, Mother, I'm starting to forget
the sound of your voice.

All I remember is
you carried me running to the boat
swarming with other escapees.

Forgive me, Mother, I'm little
by little forgetting
the smell of your hair
and the taste of your mouth.
All I remember is
I fell asleep on your back
as you carried me running
for the train crowded with other refugees.

I slept to the rocking of your steps
as you carried me,
and I woke
when you finally laid me down on the seat.
But I cried out for you to carry me.
So you laid me against your body,
and the train rocked us both,
and your voice carried me back to sleep.

The stars are blind. So is the earth.
And the moon?
What does the moon know?

Forgive me, Mother.
The more of your face I lose,
the more I stare at your photograph.

The longer I search for you in a picture,
the stranger the picture looks to me.

But I remember you carried me
farther than you ever thought
your body could carry.
And when you couldn't carry me
or yourself any farther,
you set me down.

After a little crying,
I walked the rest of the way.

To Life

Who hasn't thought, "Take me with you,"
hearing the wind go by?
And finding himself left behind, resumed
his own true version of time
on earth, a seed fallen here to die
and be born a thing promised
in the one dream
every cell of him has dreamed headlong
since infancy, every common minute has served.
Born twice, he has two mothers, one who dies, and one
the mortar in which he's tried. His double
nature cleaves his eye, splits his voice.
So if you hear him say, while he sits at the bed
of one mother, "Take me home,"
listen closer. To Life,
he says, "Keep me at heart."

The Hammock

When I lay my head in my mother's lap
I think how day hides the stars,
the way I lay hidden once, waiting
inside my mother's singing to herself. And I
    remember
how she carried me on her back
between home and the kindergarten,
once each morning and once each afternoon.

I don't know what my mother's thinking.

When my son lays his head in my lap, I wonder:
Do his father's kisses keep his father's worries
from becoming his? I think, *Dear God,* and
    remember
there are stars we haven't heard from yet:
They have so far to arrive. *Amen,*
I think, and I feel almost comforted.

I've no idea what my child is thinking.

Between two unknowns, I live my life.
Between my mother's hopes, older than I am
by coming before me, and my child's wishes, older
    than I am
by outliving me. And what's it like?
Is it a door, and good-bye on either side?
A window, and eternity on either side?
Yes, and a little singing between two great rests.

The Later Bliss

The instant my mouth first seized
onto my mother's nipple
and I tasted the warm initial
spurt of its living syllable,

I forgot everything that came before:
Heaven, God's face, my own face
before I entered time
and began to die, began to feed
upon my mother's body.

A door closed
when I closed my mouth upon her,
and I've been homesick for Heaven ever since.
So explains my friend who talks to God.

The first day my mother denied me her body,
I began another kind of forgetting.
Day after day, refusal after refusal until
the spell of our mutual desire,
along with the least memory
of our eternity together
alone, face to face,
dissolved; the pink knot
of her breast and my mouth,
that place where the branch joins the tree,
that rose of roses, unraveled.
And another door closed behind me.

But that first latch and master-fit
of two-as-one with my mother
would measure each successive

encounter on earth as no match, until I died.
Hence my melancholia.
So says my friend who claims
some sadnesses last forever.

As though my life has been
a series of doors closing behind me. A series of deeds
blindly enacting recovery of what is irretrievable.

But, O, my love, while it might be true
my mother's body was the first earth
to the later earth of my own body,

and my mother's milk the first bliss
to the later bliss of my own words
for heaven, earth, mother, milk, your body

is no mere shadow of another body.
My desires are not
the displaced desires of infancy.
All of the kisses I have given you
are not kisses meant for a forbidden first love.

Last night we lay down together
like two leaves of a door
swinging softly shut.

This morning we rise
to find the day standing open.

For a New Citizen of These United States

Forgive me for thinking I saw
the irregular postage stamp of death;
a black moth the size of my left
thumbnail is all I've trapped in the damask.
There is no need for alarm. And

there is no need for sadness, if
the rain at the window now reminds you
of nothing; not even of that
parlor, long like a nave, where cloud-shadow,
wing-shadow, where father-shadow
continually confused the light. In flight,
leaf-throng and, later, soldiers and
flags deepened those windows to submarine.

But you don't remember, I know,
so I won't mention that house where Chung hid,
Lin wizened, you languished, and Ming—
Ming hush-hushed us with small song. And since you
don't recall the missionary
bells chiming the hour, or those words whose sounds
alone exhaust the heart—*garden,*
heaven, amen—I'll mention none of it.

After all, it was just our life,
merely years in a book of years. It was
1960, and we stood with
the other families on a crowded
railroad platform. The trains came, then
the rains, and then we got separated.

And in the interval between

familiar faces, events occurred, which
one of us faithfully pencilled
in a day-book bound by a rubber band.

But birds, as you say, fly forward.
So I won't show you letters and the shawl
I've so meaninglessly preserved.
And I won't hum along, if you don't, when
our mothers sing *Nights in Shanghai.*
I won't, each Spring, each time I smell lilac,
recall my mother, patiently
stitching money inside my coat lining,
if you don't remember your mother
preparing for your own escape.

After all, it was only our
life, our life and its forgetting.

The Mother's Apple

I'm my mother's apple and that's that.
My sweetening draws death nearer, it can't be helped.
My bitterness about it is skin deep.
I'm told I'm a fourfold mystery
like the planet, but I think more.
I mean, there are tears inside me I'll never weep.
I'm heavy with unimaginable winters.
And though I'm told
apples come from apples, I believe
there must be a star somewhere among my ancestry,
and a bee, a map, a piano, and a shipwreck.
The blossoms give themselves to the wind.
Who will I be given to?
Rumor says, one day all of the iron keys
will spill out of the wind's pockets,
and each key will open a door to a mansion.
And one is named *Mind,*
and one is named *Abyss,*
and one is named *Life,*
and one is named *Work,*
and one is named *Love.*
Until then, I'll sit beneath this fragrant lintel,
the falling petals thunderous.

Section from **Furious Versions**

I wake to black
and one sound—
neither a heart
approaching nor one shoe
coming, but something
less measured, never
arriving. I wander
a house I thought I knew;
I walk the halls as if the halls
of that other
mansion, my father's heart.
I follow the sound
past a black window
where a bird sits like a blacker
question, *To where? To where? To where?*
Past my mother's room where her
knees creak, *Meaning. Meaning.*
While a rose
rattles at my ear, *Where
is your father?*
And the silent house
booms, *Gone. Long gone.*

A door jumps
out from shadows,
then jumps away. This
is what I've come to find:
the back door, unlatched.
Tooled by an insular wind, it
slams and slams
without meaning
to and without meaning.

For the Love of Less

My only mother.
Her name was Least.
Less for short.
No Single Thing
and Not at All to the world.

Sweet Nothing to her son. Sweet Nothing,
the secret heart of everything.

Less saved my life.
By the Solo River, Less found me,
and she fished me
out from among the other bodies.

Less took me home and nursed me and named me
Lacks All. Small Small. Not So Much.

Less said God gave me unto Less,
and Less could not refuse.
Better for her if she had.

Less had nothing to give,
and Less gave me all she owned.
Less had nothing to share, so Less
gave me her share of nothing.

I steeped in the deep lap of Less, staring
into her ageless smile.

I grew up under the dustless gaze of Less.
In the clean unfurnished rooms of her mind.
In that unpeopled wild, the heart of Less.

I'd hide inside Big, but Less would find me.
I'd hide inside Strong, but Less would catch me.
I'd hide inside More, but Less said, I see you.
That was our favorite game.

Less asked questions and I was forbidden to answer.
That was our other favorite game.

Who are you? Don't answer.
Where are you from? Don't answer.
Where is home? Don't answer.
What's true? Don't answer.
What's your story? Don't answer.

Is death a friend or an enemy?
Who made the world?
Are you silent from compulsion
or do you not know?

Don't answer. Don't answer. Don't answer.

What Less told me in secret
I will forever keep secret.

I wish she had never
hidden such tender shares
of her heart with me.

She should have told the birds.
They're good at keeping things to themselves.
After so many centuries, they've never given away
how they stole flying
from the Heralds and the Dominions.

She should have told the wind,
that master of secrets.

Instead, she told me.

Did Less mean to separate me
from the world
by seeding in me an opposing
center of gravity?

Did Less mean for me to grow
ever more alone in such keeping?

Even as her death is sealed
and brooks no query.

Less taught me to sort tears.
The happy tears, the sad tears,
the angry tears, the grateful tears,
the tears cried from the beginning of the world,
and the tears gathered in one lifetime.
But I never learned to sort mine from hers.

Because Less had no words of her own,
I drew pictures for Less.

Because Less had no means,
I too am bereft of means
and must wait for God
to finish this poem.

From Another Room

Who lay down at evening
and woke at night
a stranger to himself? A country

wholly unfound to himself, who wondered
behind closed eyes
if his fate meant winter knitting

outcome underground, summer
overdue, or spring's pure parable, the turning
in every turning thing, fruit and flower,
jar, spindle, and story?

He's the one who heard
the hidden dove's troubled voice
and has been asking
ever since: Whose sleep
builds and unbuilds those great rooms, Night and
    Day?

He's the one who knows
what a gleaned thing his own voice is,
something the birds
discarded, trading for a future. Call him

one whom night found beyond
the fallen gate,
where the mower never mows,
with no way to go but toward
the growing shadow of the earth.

Call him the call embarked

in search of itself, a black dew receding
unto its own beginnings.

Depending on who you ask,
his mother or his night, he's either
the offspring of his childhood or his death.

Depending on who his mother is in his dreams—
beggar, thief, boatman, mist—

he's either a man paused
on the stairs, thinking he heard
the names he used as a boy
behind his parents' house,
during evening games of lost and found,

or else a child
reading out loud to himself
from his favorite book every morning.

One day, he finds his own voice
strange, himself no longer
the names his playmates knew him by,
but not yet the boundless
quiet of his mother's watching
from another room.

Section from **Our Secret Share**

My mother hangs her small hand
on the back of my neck and leans
forward to rest her forehead to my forehead.
I hold her other hand in both of mine.
Thus we sit, breathe together,
and neither of us speaks.

Funny. There are tears a mother must singly weep.
There are tears a son must weep by himself.
There are tears a woman must unaccompanied weep.
There are tears only a man in secret can weep.

My mother lives in possession
of one part of something unspeakable,
the other part of which
I keep, her gift to me. And as long
as what she won't say
and what I'll never tell
remain our secret share
of the world's unread history,
the unspoken weds the unspoken
face to face in the silence between us,
and both of our hearts knit
to remain intact.

Both of us will have to wait
until we're each alone to weep.

The Sound of Women Weeping

It pours into the sea.
The sea brims with it, spills
over, and the foam, little bubbles
strung along myriad threads, is time.

It's different from singing,
much older
and unbroken,
an involuntary trembling,

but its vibrations no less patterned, though
its ancient warp is strung tighter,
the weft more
loosely woven, determined
by the women's ages and histories.
The loom is bone.

Their heavy sobs stain the earth and feed the roots.
Their winged keening climbs
high to wheel
before the face of the void
and is the sun.

Their weeping fills up the sky
and the sky is never filled. Empty
and full of weeping, even unto
the farthest horizon,

where the mind dies
and the heart begins its count alone
out loud, in that game without beginning,
in which the many hide

from The One, and then

the moon herds each wave home.
O, still a child, the human heart
still cries out in sleep some nights,
calling in two worlds, Here I am!
or asking in both worlds, Are you there?

but only to waken alone,
unsure if it's still a heart
or a woman weeping
or a trumpet buried
or a darkest love homing.

Don't call the heart away
from that game of games too soon.
Don't call to it at all.
Let it play

undisturbed. The rules of its game
are all that sort curse and blessing,
lost and saved,
the dark tears and the bright tears
of the women weeping.

The women weep, spinning tears.
Shuttle and heddle shine.
Spindle and bobbin shine.
Treadle and footman are dark.

The women spin,
their eyes bright with weeping,
and there's no basin but the world to catch their
    tears.

Treading, they weave. Weeping, they spin
Spinning, they fly.
Flying, they shine.

Nativity

In the dark, a child might ask, *What is the world?*
just to hear his sister
promise, *An unfinished wing of heaven,*
just to hear his brother say,
A house inside a house,
but most of all to hear his mother answer,
One more song, then you go to sleep.

How could anyone in that bed guess
the question finds its beginning
in the answer long growing
inside the one who asked, that restless boy,
the night's darling?

Later, a man lying awake,
he might ask it again,
just to hear the silence
charge him, *This night
arching over your sleepless wondering,*

*this night, the near ground
every reaching-out-to overreaches,*

just to remind himself
out of what little earth and duration,
out of what immense good-bye,
each must make a safe place of his heart,
before so strange and wild a guest
as God approaches.

Little Round

My fool asks: Do the years spell a path to later
be remembered? Who's there to read them back?

My death says: One bird knows the hour and suffers
to house its millstone-weight as song.

My night watchman lies down
in a room by the sea
and hears the water telling,
out of a thousand mouths,
the story behind his mother's sleeping face.

My eternity shrugs and yawns:
Let the stars knit and fold
inside their numbered rooms. When night asks
who I am I answer, *Your own,* and am not lonely.

My loneliness, my sleepless darling
reminds herself
the fruit that falls increases
at the speed of the body rising to meet it.

And my child? He sleeps and sleeps.

And my mother? She divides
the rice, today's portion from tomorrow's,
tomorrow's from ever after.

And my father. He faces me and rows
toward what he can't see.

And my God.
What have I done with my God?

Section from **The Herald's Wand**

2. ANY WONDER

Before
the serpent was a serpent,
she was my mother.

Living in time made me almost forget.
But I didn't forget.

She bore me into the world
from the splendor of her body with a heave,
from the sanctum of her maw with a groan,

and as she found me pleasing,
she called me Lover,
and she nursed me, singing,
Honey for the bear,
meat for the tiger,
an egg for the snake,
and milk for my baby.

Any wonder
I've been hungry and thirsty
all of my life.

Someday, I shall return
to the dark of my mother's mouth,
where all rivers meet.

Before the serpent was a serpent,
he was my father.

He brought me forth from the ancient thorn
lodged between his cloudy eye
and his incendiary eye,

and as he found me pleasing,
he called me Beloved.

And because I was no bigger
than the tip of his little finger,
he carried me on the wide brim of his hat by day.

At night, I slept in the spiral of his ear,
that gate to the unseen heard,
the unthought known,
and the garden of nutmeg.

Any wonder I've lived most of my life
insomniac by night
and distracted by eternity all day.

One day, I shall return
to rest beneath the green stem finding root
between my father's eyes,
his figuring eye and his eye of the void.

The offspring of her mouth
and of his wound.

The outcome of her darkness
and of his hurt.

Her brooding and his injury.
Her looming and his harm.
Her dwelling and his damage.

Her river and his tree.

Surrendering to divisible time,
I almost forgot.
But I never forgot.

Any wonder
I set out on earth
to learn to sing.

The Eternal Son

Someone's thinking about his mother tonight.

The wakeful son
of a parent who hardly sleeps,

the sleepless father of his own
restless child, God, is it you?
Is it me? Do you have a mother?

Who mixes flour and sugar
for your birthday cake?

Who stirs slumber and remembrance
in a song for your bedtime?

If you're the cry enjoining dawn,
who birthed you?

If you're the bell tolling night
without circumference, who rocked you?

Someone's separating
the white grains of his insomnia
from the black seeds
of his sleep.

If it isn't you, God, it must be me.

My mother's eternal son,
I can't hear the rain without thinking
it's her in the next room
folding our clothes to lay inside a suitcase.

And now she's counting her money
on the bed, the good paper
and the paper from the other country
in separate heaps.

If day comes soon, she could buy our passage.
But if our lot is the rest of the night,
we'll have to trust unseen hands
to hand us toward ever deeper sleep.

Then I'll be the crumb
at the bottom of her pocket,
and she can keep me
or sow me on the water,
as she pleases. Anyway,

she has too much to carry, she who knows
night must tell the rest of every story.

Now she's wondering about the sea.
She can't tell if the white foam laughs
I was born dark! while it spins
opposite the momentum of our dying,

or do the waves journey beyond
the name of every country
and the changing color of her hair.

And if she's weeping,
it's because she's misplaced
both of our childhoods.

And if she's humming, it's because
she's heard the name of life:

A name, but no name, the dove

bereft of memory and finally singing
how the light happened
to one who gave up
ever looking back.

In the Beginning

A woman is speaking in a place of rocks.

Her voice is the water of that place
and founds the time there.

She says the world, begun out of nothing,
stands by turning

out of grasp, a lover's *yes* and *no,*
stay and go, singing stepping
in and out of time and momentum,

the body's doctrine
of need and scarcity,

the heart's full measure
of night and day, sons and daughters.

A woman is talking. Her voice
is a boat and oars in a place of rocks.

Stranded in a rocky place,
it is a garment torn to pieces.

It is the light,
accomplished by wind and fire,
abiding inside the rocks.

A memory of the sea, it's what remains.
Homesickness in the rocks.
Homecoming in the trees.

The Moon from Any Window

The moon from any window is one part
whoever's looking.

The part I can't see
is everything my sister keeps to herself.

One part my dead brother's sleepless brow,

the other part the time I waste, the time
I won't have.

But which is the lion
killed for the sake of the honey inside him,

and which the wine, stranded
in a valley, unredeemed?

And don't forget the curtains. Don't forget the wind
in the trees, or my mother's voice saying things
that will take my whole life to come true.

One part earnest child grown tall
in his mother's doorway, and one a last look
over the shoulder before leaving.

And never forget it answers to no address,
but calls wave after wave
to a path of thirst. Never forget

the candle climbing down
without glancing back.

And what about the heart
counting alone, out loud, in that game
in which the many hide from the one?

Never forget the cry
completely hollowed of the dying one
who cried it.

Only in such pure outpouring
is there room for all this night.

Early in the Morning

While the long grain is softening
in the water, gurgling
over a low stove flame, before
the salted Winter Vegetable is sliced
for breakfast, before the birds,
my mother glides an ivory comb
through her hair, heavy
and black as calligrapher's ink.

She sits at the foot of the bed.
My father watches, listens for
the music of comb
against hair.

My mother combs,
pulls her hair back
tight, rolls it
around two fingers, pins it
in a bun to the back of her head.
For half a hundred years she has done this.
My father likes to see it like this.
He says it is kempt.

But I know
it is because of the way
my mother's hair falls
when he pulls the pins out.
Easily, like the curtains
when they untie them in the evening.

Build by Flying

I lean on a song.
I follow a story.
I keep my mother waiting
when she asks, *How long
before the wren finishes the grain?
How soon until we see
what a house the birds
build by flying?* In the dream
in which I stopped with her
under branches, on the long way home from school,
one of us, curious
about the fruit overhead, asked:
*To what port has the fragrance so lately
embarked, for whose tables?*
One of us waited for the answer.
And one went on alone,
singing. And all the place
there was grew out of listening.

Section from **The Lives of a Voice**

5. Fire Enthroned

Not another word about the dove.
Or the child, or the shadow
of the mother's voice, or the dove's voice,
or the child without a voice, or the mother's shadow,
a garment drying on the hedges

beside the river,
where the child hides, where the dove lives,
where death walks with no one watching.

Not another word about the mother's voice,
a boundless house and acre the child, spoken for, ranges,
the child without a voice, the child unspoken.

Not another word about the dove's changing pitch,
now a narrow doorway to the sea,
now an unheated room in autumn,
now a sodden bed of leaves.

The dove beside the water
builds its fine nest, does its fine math
with sticks and string and time,

confiding to the light there
what it heard
about the pollen, the nettles, the mother.

No more children's games, counting
the dove's calls and the child's cries,
keeping score for hunger and plenty.

A dove's peeled breast could barely feed a soul.
The hunger it tolls is the child's
whole inheritance.

Not another word about death,
or how the dove's tremors
are only the lapsed echoes
of that first voice, the fire enthroned,
the fire alive inside each thing
woven of dust and yearning.

Not another word about the child who,
suddenly remembering his death,
tells his mother, "By then
I'll know what to call
the color of your eyes."

Li-Young Lee is the author of six books of poetry. He has received many honors for his writing including the 2024 Ruth Lilly Poetry Prize, a Lannan Literary Award, a Whiting Award, the American Book Award, and more.

Oliver Egger is a poet, editor, and journalist. He is the editor of *I Said That Love Heals from Inside: Love Poems of Yusef Komunyakaa* (Wesleyan, 2024). He dedicates his contributions to this book to his mother, Helen Egger.

Poems in this chapbook originally appeared in the following books:

Rose (BOA, 1986): "Early in the Morning" and "I Ask My Mother to Sing"

The City in Which I Love You (BOA, 1990): "For a New Citizen of These United States" and *Section from* "Furious Versions"

Book of My Nights (BOA, 2001): "From Another Room," "Nativity," "Little Round," "In the Beginning," "Build by Flying," "The Hammock," "The Moon from Any Window," and "The Eternal Sun"

Behind My Eyes (W.W. Norton, 2008): "Mother Deluxe," "To Life," *Section from* "The Lives of a Voice, and "The Mother's Apple"

The Undressing (W.W. Norton, 2018): *Section from* "Our Secret Share"

The Invention of the Darling (W.W. Norton, 2024): "Asking Forgiveness," "For the Love of Less," *Section from* "The Herald's Wand," "The Later Bliss," and "The Sound of Women Weeping"

New and Previously Unpublished: "Infant Longing," "Mother Comfort and Who," "Pocket Catechism," "The Blessed Knot," "The Favorite," "The Inheritance," and "The Reaping"

All poems used with permission.

"Mother Deluxe," "To Life," "The Mother's Apple," "The Lives of a Voice", from *BEHIND MY EYES* by Li-Young Lee. Copyright © 2008 by Li-Young Lee. Used by permission of W. W. Norton & Company, Inc.

"Our Secret Share" from *THE UNDRESSING: POEMS* by Li-Young Lee. Copyright © 2018 by Li-Young Lee. Used by permission of W. W. Norton & Company, Inc.

"Asking Forgiveness," "For the Love of Less," "The Herald's Wand," "The Later Bliss," "The Sound of Women Weeping," from *THE IN-VENTION OF THE DARLING: POEMS* by Li-Young Lee. Used by permission of W. W. Norton & Company, Inc.

"I Ask My Mother to Sing" and "Early in the Morning" from *Rose*. Copyright © 1986 by Li-Young Lee. "For a New Citizen of These United States" and excerpts from "Furious Versions" from *The City in Which I Love You.* Copyright © 1990 by Li-Young Lee. "From Another Room," "Nativity," "Little Round," "In the Beginning," "Build by Flying," "The Hammock," "The Moon from Any Window," and "The Eternal Sun" from *Book of My Nights.* Copyright © 2001 by Li-Young Lee. All reprinted with the permission of The Permissions Company, LLC on behalf of BOA Editions, Ltd., boaeditions.org.

Special Thanks to Dianne Bilyak, Suzanna Tamminen, Stephanie Elliott Prieto, and Zahra Ashe-Simmer.

Wesleyan Chapbooks

Entanglements by Rae Armantrout

Notice by Rae Armantrout

The Poetry Witch Little Book of Spells by Annie Finch

I Will Teach You About Murder: 29 Love Poems, Edited by
Shea Fitzpatrick, Sallie Fullerton and Torii Johnson

*I Said That Love Heals from Inside: Love Poems of Yusef
Komunyakaa* by Yusef Komunyakaa, Edited by Oliver Egger

Deaths of the Poets by Kit Reed, Illustrated by Joseph W.
Reed

Dog Truths by Kit Reed, Illustrated by Joseph W. Reed

Thirty Polite Things to Say by Kit Reed, Illustrated by
Joseph W. Reed